madness like morning glories

madness

also by doris davenport

POETRY

it's like this, 1980

eat thunder & drink rain, 1982

Mangia il tuono e bevi la pioggia, 1988
    (Italian translation of *eat thunder & drink rain*)

voodoo chile / slight return, 1991

Soque Street Poems, 1995

like morning glories

poems

doris davenport

LOUISIANA STATE UNIVERSITY PRESS

BATON ROUGE

Designer: Laura Roubique Gleason
Typeface: Minion with Clarendon display
Printer and binder: Thomson-Shore, Inc.

LIBRARY OF CONGRESS CATALOGING-IN-PUBLICATION DATA

Davenport, Doris, 1949–
    Madness like morning glories : poems / Doris Davenport.
        p.   cm.
    ISBN 0-8071-2991-7 (cloth : alk. paper) — ISBN 0-8071-2992-5 (pbk. : alk. paper)
    I. Title.
    PS3604.A943M33 2005
    811'.6—dc22

                                           2004022072

The author offers grateful acknowledgment to the editors of the following publications, in which some of the poems herein have appeared previously, sometimes in slightly different form: *Asheville Poetry Review:* "Ceremony for 103 Soque Street"; *Pudding Magazine: The International Journal of Applied Poetry:* "Claude Davenport" series (ten poems). "Ceremony" appeared in *Her Words: Diverse Voices in Contemporary Appalachian Women's Poetry,* ed. Felicia Mitchell (Knoxville: University of Tennessee Press, 2002).

The following poems, some in slightly different form, were published previously in *Soque Street Poems* (Sautee-Nacoochee, GA: Sautee-Nacoochee Community Center, 1995): "Invocation," "Now I *know* you remember so and so," "Miz Fannie Mae Gibson Shueberg," "Lutesha Brown, a conjure woman with an attitude," "Mr. Arthur Wright," "Miz Maggie Wright," "Miz Amy," "Claude Davenport," "Testimonials (about Claude)," "Ethel Mae Gibson," "1002 Desota Drive, Newtown," "103 Soque," "Ceremony for 103 Soque Street," "Miz Cleo Savant," "Cornelia Regional (Colored) High School," "Sally's Cafe," "Mr. Papa Doc Williams," "Miz Zelma (Shankle) Crow," "Death on Soque," "Tanya Davenport," and "Ceremony."

For their gracious support and artistry, the author thanks Audrey Davenport, John Kollock, James Johnston, Jimmie and Richard Tinius, and the Sautee Nacoochee Community Association.

The author thanks the Georgia Council for the Arts, the Syvenna Foundation for Women, the North Carolina Arts Council, and the Kentucky Foundation for Women for their support. The author also thanks Kathryn Stripling Byer, who suggested I submit this book to LSU Press.

The title and style of "Ceremony for 103 Soque Street" were inspired by Leslie Marmon Silko's novel *Ceremony* (New York: Viking, 1977) and the title poem of Brenda Marie Osbey's *Ceremony for Minneconjoux,* Callaloo Poetry Series (Lexington: University of Kentucky, 1983).

"Hi Heel Sneakers," words and music by Robert Higginbotham © 1964, 1966 (renewed) by LILLY POND MUSIC, quoted with permission. All rights reserved.

Contents

Invocation

Sak-wi Yi

*

In the beginning, before the
beginning, words
had no meaning.

There was no beginning,
You just were, and are.
The Original Nommo
is a toy, to you.

*

Sak-wi Yi of the
Cherokee Peoples
became worded
Soquee, then Soque.
Sounds inflected
in rhythmical air,
Sak-wi Yi, village
of the First People
bound in a sacred place called
"Appalachian foothills"
in a language with no
meaning except one
arbitrarily assigned:

*

Don't mess with the Sacred.
It will get you, every time.

"Now, I *know* you remember so and so"

meaning somebody who rode through town once, ten
years ago or who lived and died before your birth. They
expect you to remember, to know, just like your mind is
their mind and if you don't, they might take it personal.
Get so mad at you, they can't get on with the story.

Not like Fannie Mae. She will get all into a story and
catch herself: "But that was before *you*
were born." Fannie Mae will pause, grin for emphasis
and say, "And I *wish* you
coulda seen it!"

not me.
when i get through
when i'm done
won't be no *wishing*
you could see.
you gone   *see.*

Miz Fannie Mae Gibson Shuebergh

(1910–2000)

Well now, I wasn't born in Gainesville, Georgia, no. But
I been here s'long it *seems* like I was, I guess. But we
lived up in Dillard and Clayton, when I was a girl, and
Cornelia, after I married. Up to me, I'd be there now! It
was *so* pretty. There was a creek we used to play in, and
Momma made the best apple pies. From our own trees!
I just *wish* you
coulda seen it.

And when John—my brother—went to the army, he
wanted an apple pie to take with him, he said. 'Course,
he couldn't, Momma being dead, by then. Never will
forget the day he went. He'd gone with the mule and
wagon, to get a chest of drawers, and he come back with
the mule—said it was time to go. I asked him for a dime,
and could I go with him. He said he didn't have a dime
and I couldn't. I was just too outdone, with him! The
mule's name? No, I *don't* remember but do you know, if
your pants legs get any higher, you will have to have a
party and invite them down to see your shoes!

'Course now, you never know what people see in each
other—a man and a woman. You never do know, do
you? And whatever it is *they* see, they can't make you
see it!
They can't. Half the time, why—they don't know
themselves! And I have got a *lot* of nieces and nephews
and I love them all. Will & Kate's, John & Elvie's,
Jesse's, Lula's. Why, I got *great* nieces and nephews.
But, what I mean—they all grown. Or, they *think* they
grown. And they don't pay me any more attention than
the man in the moon. Matter of fact, they'd probably pay
more attention to *him*—just because they Gibsons, and
all Gibsons are stubborn.

Still, I didn't think it was a good idea for my niece Ethel
Mae (that Mae in her name's after me) to marry Claude.

But—she was grown, by then! So, they got married, and
when she had her first baby, I was there and it's a good
thing!

That sorry Claude was drunk; he was *always* drunk,
look like. No—I never had any children but *any fool*
would know what to do. Any fool, that is, except Claude.
Out in the yard—cold as it was, *crying* and talking
to his fool self. Peoples, I came as close to killing a man
then as I ever did in my life. Told him I'd slap him into
next *year* (and it was January) if he didn't get out that
yard, and get Greenlee or Dr. Butler. And then, when
Greenlee got there—and she took her time coming—
you'd have thought this
was her first baby, too!

Been delivering babies since *she* was a baby, but
I had to help her. I had a *time* that night and every time I
told Greenlee something, I had to say it twice! Well,
the baby got born, like they gen'ly do, and I watched
everything that silly nurse did. (Dizzy as she was,
somebody had to watch her.) So, I saw the baby come;
saw it had a veil, which didn't surprise me, since I come
here with a veil, at least that's what they say. (Used to
be a lot of babies born like that.)

If you can't believe your own momma, who *can* you
believe? My mother (God rest her soul) said I came
with a veil. She told me what it looked like—that's how I
knowed what I was looking at. That silly nurse acted
like she saw a big snake.
So I told her what it was, and about *my* veil, and it was
cold that night, but it was *colder* the night I was born.
Least, that's what they tell me. But—people don't
appreciate what you do for them. Still, I do what I can
for my kin. And I still say, it was a good thing
I was there that night. Else, *that* niece
might not've got here.

Lutesha Brown
a conjure woman with an attitude

They called me a two-headed woman when I was just a girl.
Called me two-headed when I was too young to know what
that meant, but I found out. I found out.

When I got to Gainesville—never you mind now from where—
I liked it. I set up my practice, put out the word
and the sign: a red hand. Some silly kids called me
"The Red Lady" (but really I am quite black). Some
close friends called me "Red." My customers, though, called me
"Miz Lutesha, ma'am" and at that, they better
say it right or I would *see* red in a minute and
fix it so they couldn't see nothing else.
I useta warn people—"Don't trouble the Spirits.
Don't you *think* about getting on my nerves."
But some would. Dojesus, some just would.

They *knew* I was a two-headed woman and was glad about it.
They knew, but this one—Claude. Y'all know him.
Got in my face, and both me and him thought he was cute.
I *will* say that. Well, we was friends at first.
I'd listen to him tell his dreams.
He wanted him a good woman, not like his ma.
Wanted a house full of boys but then he
changed his tune. And mine.

Even a two-headed woman can get weak in the head
(and the knees) sometimes. Well, things happened like they happened.
He sung that tune all the way into my bed,
then changed it, again.
Said he just wondered what a conjure
woman's . . . was like.
He said that, to my face, and laughed.

I saw red so bright, I thought my brain had exploded.
All the Spirits was troubled, some mad at me.

I saw red, heard red, tasted red, choking me.
Claude now, getting dressed, telling me this
woman he found in Cornelia, how she gone have all
these *boys* for him. And
my throat eased up and I laughed. And laughed.

Girls is all he got off that woman. I didn't touch *her*—she was
under Clio's hand—but I fixed him. Even acted friends with him,
so I could hear *all* about it. How he couldn't stop drinking.
Couldn't keep a job. Didn't understand
his wife (and couldn't treat her right).
Couldn't get no boys. I still saw red. And kept laughing.

He brought his kids to see me once. (He showed them like
prize pigs.) The oldest one wore a red jacket.

I pointed at her, said "Don't you *ever* come around me
wearing red! Don't you never wear red again!"
But it wasn't just the color, it was the Sight.
She had it and I could see in her
my competition. That's if I let her be.
She scared me (so I had to scare her) and
she was only about six.
Well, Claude I fixed.
He had bad, bad, blood-red dreams. He died,
in his own red blood, in the street, near my house.
He knew, as he died, why and who done it. And even *now*
he ain't got no peace.

Marie Duvalle (Witch Marie La Strega)

It bothered me until I got to where I could ignore
foolishness. But it *did* gripe me awhile—how people took up
with Tesha, and wouldn't, unless they had to or was
new in town, have that much to do with me. She was just
a girl, a baby, to me. I was grown when she came here.
I let rooms to young married couples
til they got straight. I ran a store on this side of town, up at the
corner near Joe Harris' farm (the Goat Man).
I was a long, longtime part of this town.
But what they call me?
Witch.

And I tried to tell Lutesha about that boy. Told
her I'd seen the Signs, said he would never do
nothing right and—it wasn't even his fault. Some bad evil
touched him the day he was born. I saw his birth (and death) in
the face of that young Fannie Mae, when her
and her husband Johnny stayed with me.

That's what I do. Read signs, and if you know how,
if you got the gift, signs are everywhere. And when I first saw
Fannie Mae's face, I read
that she'd never *give* birth. Saw her niece's lines
crossed up with that evil in Claude, and *their* children crossed
up too. Lutesha's power went to her head. Talking about *she*
fixed Claude. Something fixed him *way* before her. Well, after
what happened happened, me and Tesha wasn't friends no more.
I miss her. But I saw that coming too.
Just like I can look in a jar of dill pickles
and see Clio's Work, up the road.

Nurse Marsha Greenlee

Babies can pick the *worse* times to come.
Wait til you trying to rest, soaking y'r feet, or eating some
good barbecue. But I loved my work. Dr. E. E. Butler, my
boss, was one of the best men ever lived.
Back then, it was natural to do the Work and deliver babies
too. And if I do say so myself, I was good at bringing babies.
Still, I never *will* forget that one January of 19 and 49. How
cold it was, how so many babies kept coming, way out in the
country. Round the end of the month, I was wore out, ready
to sleep a month.

Finally I laid down late one night, settled in, and here come
somebody yelling: "Hey!! Hey!! I say hey, in there, with
your fine self. We need help. My wife fixing to have my boy!"
Wasn't nobody but Claude, drunk (as usual), steady banging
on my door. If I hadn't felt sorry for his wife—if I hadn't loved
babies—I would be laying there now. But I got on up and went
over to Newtown.

His wife was doing alright even if it was her first. Her aunt,
Fannie Mae, was with her, and *she* liked to made me loose my
religion. Sat there going on and on about how sorry Claude
was. Didn't have no food *nor* electricity in the house, she said,
and she had to promise to slap Claude just to make him come
and get me (and her so little, a mosquito would slap harder), she
said. OH, she could talk. And I'm trying to see to the birthing,
and see what all these Spirits want, floating around.

Early next morning, about five, the mother was knocked out;
Claude had been done passed out, so it was just Miz Fan and
me. The girlbaby finally came and Fannie Mae at least shut up
for *that.* I moved as fast as I could, but she saw it. The baby had
a caul. I saw it, took it, and destroyed it. (That aggravating
woman going "Ooooh. It's born like me. 'Least, they *say* I
came here with a veil" and on and on about the weather when
she was born. Like she knew. Like I cared.)

Yes, destroyed it because I could *see*—with the parents she had,
she would have a *hard* life. She didn't need the Spirits
messing with her too and though I loved the Work it was more
than a notion. A person had to be *ready* for that.

Next thing I know, Marie asking "What'd you do with it?" Her
and Tesha had been quit talking, but up til then, we was still
friends. Marie got all salty about it. Said I had no business to
do that; that I'd done more harm than good—so we fell out too,
over that. I did what I thought was right.
Enough of us had the Sight, and still couldn't see straight. But
if I'd known more—like Marie did—
I might have done different.
Nothing could've made that baby's life no harder.
No easier, either.

Mr. Arthur Wright

(1873–1961)

They didn't *ask* to be born.
Not Claude's, and nobody else's. They don't
need *that* much—a roof
over their heads, some beans, some love.

I wasn't born in slavery, but
close enough to see
what it did to the little ones.
Hurt me, so bad.
No, I never had any children of my
own, though I did want some.

I don't have a lot to say about my life.
I did what I had to, to get by, like we all do
and when I married
Miz Maggie Wright, I had *been* a
grown man. Had done *some* living. But it was
her I wanted to settle with. And I
didn't have a lot of kin
so it was easy to take up with hers. Her sister Susie and
her husband. Her grown daughter Amy. Amy's boy,
Claude, though, took *some*
getting used to. And I
can't say I ever did—get used to Claude.

If you gone keep having
babies—I useta tell him—
at *least* take care of them.
And his little girls was
just like all kids.
Needed some food, some love and
they was easy to love. At least, for me.
I—we—didn't do no more than
anybody else would've done.
I just wish

I'd knowed enough
to *write* a will
to leave the oldest
girl my house.

Miz Maggie Wright

(1883–1968)

Always liked children, wanted lots of my own but my first husband—they
say I had lots of husbands but I just had two—my first husband had something
else on his mind. And it wasn't til *after* I married him that I knew.
I can see him just as plain, even now. He had a strong, clear singing voice, and
a pretty smile. First time I saw him, he was smiling and singing. Claimed
when he first saw me, he knew he was gone have me. For life.

Said he'd worked roots for me. I knew some people did that
for a living but I thought he was just talking—you know how men do. *But,*
after we got married, he kept talking and acting strange. Wore me out with
his dreams and trying to make me tell mine. One time, I couldn't sleep for a
week, he worried me so. I'm surprised we had one child, way he carried on.
And by then, I'd had enough of *him,* for life. So when my grandson had his
kids, well, it was like they was mine.

Arthur Wright was a sweet man. (He always called me Miz Maggie Wright.)
Just like he loved me—and overlooked it when I took a nip now and then—he
loved my peoples. We just treated Claude's like they was ours.

Miz Amy

(1904–1957)

I told people he was gone wind up
on the chain gang before he got to
first grade if somebody didn't kill him first. Because he
was a bad child from the time he was born. I had a *bad*
time with Claude's daddy, Claude Senior. I had a *bad*
time, having Claude Junior. And it got worse after that.
And you right. He got that honest
from me. Folks call Claude uppity but they ain't seen
nothing. Shoulda seen me in my day, way I
useta strut around. I was *some* kinda fine and
didn't care who I let know it. Was a
deep-bone sweet chocolate brown til they put me in the
ground and *stayed that way!!* Miz Maggie Wright
couldn't do nothing with me. I couldn't do
nothing with Claude. I was born loving a good time and no-
good, good-looking, good-loving men. Which is what
Claude's daddy was: no-good, and at that, hi yaller.

Don't know why I married him (coulda had my pick).
We fought so much, it's a wonder Claude
wasn't born dead. See, Claude's daddy didn't want him—
didn't want me to have him—and *that's* why I named the
boy Junior, for spite, and even better, Claude was dark
complected, like me. Didn't look nothing like that ole
yaller dawg and *he* tried to say that wasn't his baby but
I knowed, and he knowed, it was. But, oooh wee, we'd
fight! Especially once I started drinking, and *once* I
started, I kept on going. Then, how he *looked* made me
mad. His face wasn't put together to suit me so I let him
know it. By the time

Claude Junior was five, we'd split up for good but, chile,
we fought. Except a few breaks to eat, sleep, and the 17
hours it took me to have his baby, we fought and
Claude Jr. saw it, too.

Claude was four that day.
The doctor was tall, heavyset, yaller.
And Claude spied him coming up the path,
lit out running at him. Claude Jr. *did*
stab the doctor
in his thigh. But then he said,
"I'm sorry. I thought
you was my daddy. I'm gone kill my daddy."

Claude Davenport

(1928[?]–1964)

In the first place,
I was *born* in Atlanta,
not in this little dump. Let's
get that straight, first. And yeah, I drink much
likker as I want to. I'm a grown man, don't take no
stuff from nobody. Never have, never will.

And I like me some fine women
with big behinds. That's the first
thing I noticed about my wife. (In the Navy?
I was just a cook, but a damn *good* cook.
I'll make you some of my raw oyster stew, one day.)

Well, I don't know if I planned to marry
her but she wouldn't give it up unless
I married her. Then soon's I touched
her, she got pregnant but I still say
that first baby she had ain't mine. (Too
light-complected to be mine.)

Shiiiit. I know when I'm lying, and I
do it anyway. I say, I *know*
I'm lying, but that don't give
you the right to contradict nothing I say.
"Claude got the Devil in him," Amy use to say. Huh.
The devil *wish* he had some of what I got. Hell
—don't care if Slim had twenty
kids (which I thought
she just might), they'd be
mine. They better be. They'd
have to be. I don't give her
time to fool with nobody but
me. I—I ain't got to talk about
me. Ask anybody.

Testimonials (about Claude)

1

Ah yes. Here is another example of the kind of random and irrevocable
destruction Amerika offers to a Black man in the twentieth century. (An
Amerika, I might add, built on a slave-based capitalism which, parasitically,
and thereafter, required Black males' denigration and exploitation.)
Obviously, like innumerable others, he was psychologically and emotionally
castrated by systemic racism, hence felt inadequate, and bereft of his symbolic
a classic and tragic case of displacement and he transferred his pent up *rage*
and justifiable frustration onto his spouse in a classic case that demonstrates
the emascu

2

SAY   WHAT?
Say what?
Way you talking, you didn't
even *know* the biscuit eater.
He was evil. He beat his wife for fun.
He f——d over everybody,
for the pure de meanness of it!

3

Don't care what nobody say,
he did love his wife, *and* all
them kids. Just didn't know
how to show it, how to let
them know it.

4

Yeah. I knew him. Could not stand him.
And I am a Christian,
a God-fearing man (unlike
some others around here
sneaking off in the woods
on Saturday night practicing voodoo then
in church on Godsday)
and I mean, Claude
could make   me   forget

my   religion! And I am not
proud of this—but if I saw him coming
I would cross the street and
stay crossed, for at *least* a week.

                    5

He was *not* born in Atlanta; his *daddy* was from Atlanta but I knowed
his momma, name was Amy. She *and* her momma, wasn't from
nowhere else but Gainesville. Little bitty Gainesville all day long. All
night long, too. Now!

                    6

I knew Claude; I was one of his women.
                    I went to his funeral. I cried.
                    I loved him.

                    7

Just to look at, a few years before, she wasn't much to see.
Just one of Elvie's and John's, and Miz Shueberg's niece. She
was tall and skinny then, one day—greatjoobalooba!

She got a little taller, kept a tiny tiny waist, but then
the rest just . . . tapered down to little fine legs, and
everything fit! From her long, wavy black hair, and her
momma's lightbrown complexion; big clear eyes and pretty
white teeth, with a gap in 'em, down to her feet. All they kids
was good-looking but I swear, tell you something I never told
nobody else. I believe *God* made that girl, deliberate.

What's that? Hell, naw, I ain't colorstruck. But maybe God is!
I say, God created ALL Negro women, all they colors,
to keep my eyes happy, let me know what
kinda woman I oughta look for, or at least, look *at!*
Some say she was a little stuck-up
but if she was, she had a reason or
two. Anybody with eyes in his head
would have wanted her. For keeps.
She'd make men dream dreams, and see visions!
Yeah. She was—ahhhh. Y'all know what I'm talking about.
No wonder ole Claude Jr. wanted to marry her.

Ethel Mae Gibson

I visited my aunt Fannie Mae in Gainesville as
much as I could to get away from home. The first time
I saw him I thought he was stuck on hisself. He acted
like "I'm God's gift to women, and you know it, too."
Still, he was cute.
He'd been around the world, in the Navy, also to Atlanta.
I'd mainly been to Clarkesville and Clayton and I was
just seventeen. Even with Daddy following right behind
us, Claude talked his stuff.
I tried to act like it didn't faze me none, but it did. It did.
Made my bobby socks roll up and down.

"Slim," he'd say—that was his nickname for me—
"Slim, you got the key to the kingdom" and
"The woman who can beat yo' time ain't been born
and her momma's dead."
I like riddles. Sounded like a riddle to me so I giggled.
I liked how he talked.
I liked how he looked. I liked how he looked to me
and looked at me.
And that's all there was, to that.

1002 Desota Drive, Newtown

(Miz Maggie Wright and Mr. Arthur Wright: Granny & Grandpa)

at the top of one hill and the bottom of
another street unpaved dusty red
dogwood trees, a big flower garden in front

train tracks, across
a deep grassy ditch. At train time, when Momma
went from Gainesville to Cornelia
Grandpa & Granny & Daddy stood
in the backyard waving at us
waving back on the train (Grandpa waved a red bandanna)

sometimes i stand there with them
wave at Momma and my
sisters heading north
somebody still

   stands there waving
        &
        waiting

103 Soque

According to Daddy John Gibson, when we first met
i said, "You ain't my grampa. He in Gainesville."
Momma said, when i first saw the
electric bulb hanging from the front room ceiling,
i got scared. Pointed, asked
"What *is* that?" (at our house on Collins Street
only kerosene lamps.)

103 Soque Street. A four-room wooden high-ceilinged
white house at the foot of a hill
behind a ditch of red dirt, house full of
light, noise and more people than i
ever saw before
laughing, pinching, poking me. my "she-won't-smile"
ten aunts and uncles, *and* a ghost. 103 Soque. Soquee.

Ceremony for 103 Soque Street

Soque is a Cherokee word turned Black on the Hill
across the railroad track, in Appalachian foothills where
madness like morning glories took over everyone trying to be
insane and acceptable all the time and all the while, hainted.
Two rows of houses along the railroad track
Mr. Oscar Wise, the Peanut Man, and his family
still there in the air and honeysuckles, hainted.
Mack, our cousin, said he saw a casket roll down Soque,
stop in front of 103 and roll back up the hill again.

Mr. Miller's wife, and that's all the name she had, been dead
for years but we saw her pale, pale face surrounded by wild
colored-Indian black hair pressed against the window pane. At
103 Soque, in the bedroom where 10 people slept, a square
hole in the ceiling. From that hole, one night, a man in white
floated down, ate the lightbulb, floated back up. Anthony and
Jeff, 20 years later, saw the lightbulb dance up and down.
Instantly sober they split. Some of this ain't acceptable.
Some of it *wasn't* acceptable. But we got a permit.
Now.

Fish said the man Jimmy saw, sitting over the middle of the well,
with no head was his great-granddaddy. He got his head cut off.

*

Near no ocean, just Russell Lake, the other side of and down
a steep mountain. Nothing to cause this fog. Thick, wet
blinding fog when fall softened the already quiet hill leaves
fell muffled & slow in animated fog. In that fog

they dream silence dreaming each other. In that fog, one
walked out alone at night, never told what she saw
but Miz Clio knew the fog in the trees, in & out the leaves,
winds with wordless voices, distinct, endless. The red dirt
hums, pine trees chant the background calling.

Red dirt reaches up, the trees down
meet in people's minds
in the same dream. Dreaming they are real.

Outsiders and foreigners from Atlanta claim disbelief.
Laugh at a big red apple for a downtown monument; say no
highways come near us so we don't exist to them who can't
touch a belief that recreates each other, each day and in sleep,
dream the same dreams.
Red dirt inflected pine trees scented dreams.

*

We shared dreams & short memories. dreams, memories and
amnesia. At the end of school we always "went somewhere"
a bus full of excited children in May headed to the
Indian Reservation in North Carolina
each time like the first time, except a few jaded ones
("Oh shoot! The Indians *again?*") but

WE   were a
reservation, on Cherokee land. On a beautiful hill of
apartheid, reserved for "the coloreds" and though
many of us honestly had Indian blood
we had short memories, dreams and amnesia.

The Cherokee *could* have traveled to Northeast Georgia
to see *us* making, not beads and moccasins, no Touristy
Attractive stuff, just inventing each other repeatedly on Soque
Street with names like Wolf. Drunk Dessa. Mr. Rat. Mr.
"Poppa" Doc. Mr. Jim Smith.
"The Elephant Killer," Miz Zelma. Miz Clio. To see our
ritual stompdowns you'd find Sally's Lunchroom,
Fred's Tavern or another juke joint way, way back
in the woods with permission (and a guide)
and then . . .

Miz Clio Savant

(1883–present)

It seemed like I was "chained and bound"
like that song says. Oh I listen to this
blues stuff if nobody is around.
Alone, I listen.

What *you* know about it? Nothing.

> By the time we got to Banks County, it
> was hard enough. Bad enough,
> leaving Charleston. But Jehru—
> my brother—had to leave for messing with
> the wrong man's daughter.
> And I was *some* tired riding, riding, riding that wagon up
> into pine trees, hills, mountains and a few funny
> talking people by the time we got to that
> hill in Cornelia,
> I told Jehru this was the place.
> If he'd do like I say this was it.

*

> Hot-hot that day, playing out
> back with my five sisters
> half naked too young to cover what
> we didn't have. And that raggedy doll two of my
> sisters fighting over, so hot it almost
> melt, I laughing, don't want that doll
> noway except to bury it maybe
> poke sticks in glassy no-color eyes
> another sister singing
> one just yelling like any other
> summer day
> but then I see
> our momma sister, Aunt Zese
> quiet-quiet in too much white
> clothes she always wear
> stand there, stare us silent;
> silent too, my momma with her.

Aunt Zese point slow, raise her arm
her finger at me, "She the one."
I start crying
saying Momma it not me. It
them—making fight over ugly doll,
making noise, *NOT* me!

"Shhh," Momma say. "Come on in the house."
She look at my aunt—aunt look back
at her; nod. I go.
I go to Aunt Zese house and I—what I know—
almost ten. From that day,
that heat still on me now,
I live with my Aunt Zese, in her house, on her
island off Charleston.

When the moon full up we do certain thing.
Moon gone, sky dark-dark I
do other things
Aunt Zese tell me sometimes know
what to do without her.
I do what she say, and don't. I grow.
They say in town
Clio the one. She see she talk with
the Spirits.

Other full moons we dance. Aunt Zese
make the movements
my body follow words, chants
drums, not many
years later I am what
my Aunt Zese said. I was the one.
I am   the one.

The men came, after the boys. They came,
when my aunt said and after
she gone, I stayed. The men came, with
drums, with words—

how I don't need no mo'
power except what I got
all over Charleston they wait for the
day I boat over to
see Momma, to market,
all the men wait &
watch me walk—women too.
They knew. I was the one.

And I could see, knew how I looked, coming and going
rich black skin, deep-set eyes full
lips; long, long arms and legs smooth walk so
there *were* men, on my island.
For the work, for the Spirits,
they came. They left but
Dina stayed.

Another hot-*hot* this one day I
had done all the things
fixed all and sent them home
so evening, night. I
listened to tree frogs talk to lightning bugs,
small waves slap
my porch; plenty stars but new moon, dark-dark
like I like it. I take a
deep breath and get comfortable to
set a spell when I
hear soft boat sounds, steady coming.
Who *now* I think, aggravated, who *now*
giving birth, bleeding to death, wanting
love fixed and a soft voice

"Clio?"
the way she said my name
asking, but telling me too.
I know her voice, her eyes, her thighs. She
dance the Spirits in too. Honey-sweet, her voice.
She came, soft, on my porch

stood quiet, look a question and answer
at me we neither one spoke I
stood. Went to her. Took Dina's hand.
Went in my cabin.

I was the one. She stayed and
we stayed like that for a long, long
time until she died. I would still
be there. Except for my brother, Jehru

was the reason I left. He, the only son,
after six girl-wimmin. He, with no
power except what little Momma had
left after us.
He claimed he was a seventh
son but he was not (I was the one). He
was just baby boy to us, and he stayed a
boy, a baby to me and because he
was a baby, and because I was the one, I
was the one got on
that wagon to save his trifling life.

*

Don't even remember why we headed for North Georgia
except it had to be a ways from
the two-headed doctor's daughter
and I had to go to
save his life. And brought the
Spirits saw this red dirt and mixed in.
Mixed me in with it. But I

was some tired, halfway
evil at first. This little no-sidewalk place
people in shacks and no conjure womon, except
one back in the woods, power shriveled up
but I paid my respects.
We live in the big yellow

house at the crossroads
of Second and Soque.

And I work them all. Got us all
dreaming the same dream like
Dina in my blood.
All I felt for my Dina, they feel for each other, and
other things I never felt for nobody. I fixed us
and anybody else come through here, too.

"Deacon J," my brother became and all anybody
said, except maybe Zelma and
two more, I was just "Deacon's sister."

My walk was the same
even if I went not much further
than church and back. My feet remembered
the drums, the ocean. There even was a few women
walked smooth like me—even
little girls—but no Dina. I talked to
the Spirits and haints all up on the hill.

It *looked* like I was bound, and chained.
My spirit, it was free.

*. . . and you are to hear these all speaking at once like somebody opened a tightly
sealed jar of peach preserves gone bad or a jar of wasps*

I always knowed Miz Clio was a bull dyke / uh huh, knowed she was funny / y'all
make me *tired*. just cause she didn't want nunna the sorry men y'all had / lot of
nerve *she* got! / it ain't her bizness to tell nothing / she ain't even *from* Cornelia /
ANY of y'all from Cornelia? man, you ain't nothing but a apple knocker, no way /
and you just a sooner, y'self. / if she just *got* to say something, I wish she'd tell /
y'all just jealous. always was. / me? me?! I could whup her ass right now she ain't
nothing to me / Jealous? Jealous? What she got for us to be jealous of? / Well, she /

Cornelia Regional (Colored) High School

(located on the Hill in Habersham County where African Americans, grades 1st through 12th, were bused from four contiguous counties— Banks, Habersham, Rabun and White)

1

The Bean Creek Rabun County school bus
never did get in until after the
Lord's Prayer and the Pledge Allegiance.
We could count on it. Or they'd hold
the pledge and prayer until Rabun got in
or didn't if it was a bad
freeze up the mountains or if it was farming time.
(Don't know what they farmed. Pine trees? Clouds?)
When they got in, we watched them to see
whatever we could see. Oh—the *people*
were mainly pretty but we *did* grow some
ugly up in these hills and we'd wait for *them*
to come, to see if they'd got any uglier since yesterday.

2

Lunchtime. Time of intense terror and
joy. Joy because Miz Maggie Dover could
lowmo' cook. For a quarter (if not,
baloney on white bread in a greasy
brown paper sack, dry peanut butter or
a cold fatback sandwich) and if
you *had* a quarter you got
Miz Maggie's lunch:

Fried fish, rolls, chicken & dumplings, stewed
chicken, Brunswick stew, cornbread &
greens. Peach cobbler, with real
crisp brown dough on top every day
like Sunday except for
the terror: one of them girls
from Across the Ditch

might take your quarter or
your lunch after you paid for it and
slap your face, too.

3 *(flashback from A.H.)*

I have never had
enough to eat.
No matter how
much I eat, it ain't—is not—
enough. And I know
good and well it's because
of Miz Maggie's; how good
her food *looked*   that I
rarely got to taste because —— took it. Yes
it *was* a long time ago but *still*
nothing like that here in New York.
After a while I just gave —— my quarter
to save her the trouble of beating on me
and save me the *extra* pain of seeing what
I could not touch. Taste. Seem like
I ain't *never* had enough
to eat since.

4

Friday afternoon one-hour "socials."
A record player, the latest 45s
and a few oldies; the boys played with boys,
the girls danced with girls, in fourth and fifth grades
the teachers changed records, watched us,
checked watches
waiting   for time   to go.

Miz Sara Mae Pennix / Mrs. S. M. Cook

Well, I got assigned to Cornelia Regional just out of college and
couldn't say no. I needed the job. Momma, back home in North
Carolina, needed the money. Besides I wanted that job and I wanted
to be a credit to the race, and where it would do some good as far as I
could and God-willing. But these folk was heathens! Oh they had
church, two here and one in Mt. Airy and Rev. Strickland preached
hard at them every second and fourth Sunday at Shady Grove but the
people—just wild. I thought. But I look back, and have to laugh. I
once told my students (3rd through 5th grades) to change the bed
sheets once a week. That I planned to check, just walk in, throw back
the covers, and look. I had *some* nerve.
But then, I found me a sweetie, Garland. I married him. The dirt was
red, like back home. The hills, the air, and everybody was right
friendly. (Wild though.) I loved my students. Even now, I can
see in my mind how that first group sat in the classroom. Well,
before long I was one of them "heathens." I have taught school here
for almost fifty years! And lived here—Cook and me, our two
children—at the top of Soque, just as long. I was assigned to Cornelia
but then, well, I guess I'd just call it love. And I'm just very thankful
for how the Lord have brought me out.

Miss Robbie Mae Franklin
(February 13, 1932–April 7, 2003)

You cannot get too familiar with some people.
If you play with a puppy, it will lick you in the face.
And I made *sure* these little people understood *that*
about me. My students were all
afraid of me—as they should have been.
A few of them hated me or, thought they did.
As an alumnus of South Carolina State, I had high, *high*
standards to uphold; my students as well.
        They cringed, when they came to
me for high school English and
French. Oh I heard their little stories; I

laughed in their faces. A few of them truly
fascinated me. Uh huh. They really did.

Indeed, I had high standards! Appearance to
deportment, it was imperative that I
did and I taught them by
precept and by example, the way I carried
myself and dressed (because all of
my sorors and I were known for looking good.
Uhhh huh, we really were). Unlike some others,
I socialized only with those in my class, not with
those for whom I wished to set an example.
Familiarity breeds contempt, so I had my
Chivas Regal with Sara Mae or another peer; I
never socialized with my children. But I taught.
Oh yes. I taught, and I'd tell them,
"You're gone remember
Robbie M. Franklin." And right now,
most of them on the hill
would thank me for it.

Mr. M.

What they need is a football team. Never
heard of a high school
without one . . . and but
they got   some   fine
women   up   here!
You hear me? Some *fine*
women—even the schoolteachers
look good—but this local stuff! Never seen
such . . .   They need a football team.
I need me some of these women.

                    Mr. T.

            Shit.   I need a drink.
            People strange down in
            South Georgia where I'm from—

but *these!* Some these women look
like they could put spells
on you that even God can't take off. I did not
finish college just to get hoodooed
by some strange upcountry woman.
Pour me a shot. Straight up.
(Plus they crazy. The children too.
Like that one, stretched out on the girls'
bathroom floor, said she *counting* the
tiles.) Make that   a double.

Miss Phillips

At least I tried to teach Home Economics. Everybody needs
to know how to eat better, not just more. Nutrition,
the five basic food groups, and sewing, were the subjects I taught. So
the girls would know how to make things for themselves. (Some of them really
wore their skirts too tight, too short.) Things that looked decent and fit right.
Most *wouldn't* sew a straight seam. They tried to aggravate me, especially that
Gibson boy, but I didn't let them. I just didn't.

Mr. K.

My nephew Esau has been
living off me most
of his natural life—
some of you,
you just like him.
Trifling. Just trifling.
And if you can't
learn or you won't,
what *are* you good for?
History and Industrial Arts
make a *good* foundation
for a good life. But you all
hardheaded. Just like that
sorry Esau.

and Rev. D.

Heehee hee. Heeheehee. The Atlanta Interdenominational
Theological Center did *not* produce no fools! I said, it did NOT
produce no fools! Now me, I got to know
these strange people and I—I
found them amusing, and found
the Lord had my work cut *out* for me!

Even with two jobs (science teacher *and* AME preacher) I was
not making anything. As they would say, "not nothing."
Why, if the women didn't cook (I said cook, not *look.*
Heeheehee)

so good, it wouldn't have been worth it but I *loved* aggravating
those kids. Ignorant people have been a source of inexpensive
amusement for me all my life. Now, they might laugh at me
because I am very, very Black—and I know it and am proud of it
—and I am also very, very fat—which I also know, and do not
mind, as I love myself some of all the food that my God ever
made, and love of food runs in my family. (Just look at my
parents.) Still, I built them a new church.

I love a good laugh and that is just what those country people
were to me: a good joke, in the name of the Lord. They laughed
at me. I know they talked about me, *worse* than they talked about
our Lord and Savior Jesus C. but oh—
they made the best fried chicken, up on that hill. The best.

the principal

In 1958, the first year I came here, I told my wife
these people need *educating* and
if it takes the rest of my life, I will do it.
They needed teaching, bad. No kind of morals.
Look how the women walk and most of them don't
even wear underclothes. Having babies

for anybody. By the time they're fifteen
they could have five. And the men!
Just dogs. No-good dogs. But
everybody knows they can't act that way
unless the women let them, so just
looking at some of these young women, soon
after we got here, inspired me.
That spring and every spring, I lectured on how
they ought *not* to behave: like a bitch-dog
in heat, going off in the woods. HAH!
That, some algebra, a little Latin (but my wife's right; they
don't need *that* here), Booker T. and morals. And then, seemed
like it was my sole duty to save that one little Gibson girl.
The way she acted, how she walked, and barely eleven. Sure, she was
book smart. She even taught her classmates algebra, but: no common sense.
No moral sense. And her mother—five or six kids and no
husband that I ever saw or heard of. The girl needed education
and *guidance.* Else, she'd end up just like her maw!

                                        . . . and here *they* come:

She sho' got some *fine* hairy legs! / Aw, man, she a teacher / Well, all I said is she
got some fine legs. What's wrong with that? / Better not let *her* hear you say that /
Yeah—do, and you WON'T HAVE NO LEGS! / Aw, she like me. / She ain't got to
be so stuck up. / Who she think she is, nohow? / She got to use the bathroom, just
like everybody else . . . / Ah, y'all make me tired! Her and the rest just trying to do
something for the hill. / Y'all ain't nothin but crabs in a barrel / Yeah—least they
tryin! / Yeah—most other folk woulda been done left here / But still and all, he
ain't got no bizness talkn bout us like he do. What *he* know about it—he be up
there calling us dawgs / and y'all ain't got no better sense than to laugh. / All y'all
hush. Just shut up.

The Egotistical Sublime

was invented in Northeast Georgia shortly
after the hill was settled
by people soon to be
kin by sharing, essentially,
the same skin
never knowing that
that was it: "I."
I exist, therefore you do.
I think—therefore you are—if I think about
you. (The Nommo power of "I ain't
thinkin' about you."
Cruel finality of
"Forget *you*.")
not knowing they could
not *not*   think
about each other,
and in that (delusion),
sublime.

Church

1 *Miz Kamunete Mouf*

The BYPTU at Shady Grove, the Baptist Young People's Training every Sunday evening around 6 p.m. Lawd *knows* these younguns need training; most of them have no manners, in church or out and I don't see how Mary Turk—bless her heart—can put up with them the way she do every Sunday. Me, I know I wouldn't but then, by her living alone—no kids, no husband (her and Ernest *been* separated) just a few lady teachers stay with her and she *do* keep herself looking good! Wear some of the prettiest hats, too, steady smoking her Winstons. And got a nice shape, and you know, she can't be *that* old, nohow; she don't just teach BTU—look how she *always* teaching them! Some of them if they leave home, soon's they get back, they ask about her, go see her. They do say that it was Mary and a few more *ran* the church. Beulah, they say, wrote Rev. Strickland's sermons or at least told him what to preach about, especially somebody she didn't like, or done something she didn't like. Why, it *do* have something to do with Mary! Her and Beulah was best friends! Wasn't they?—Or was it them that couldn't stand each other?

2 *Miz Mary Turk*

They needed something to do; and living and working close with all the teachers, over the years, I *knew* that. I always told them, *make* something of yourself. And BTU was fun. Sure, it was *work,* but I didn't mind. The young people got a chance to be with each other. Sing, discuss scriptures. Plan little fund-raising projects . . . and they were fun, most of them. But I was just crazy about 'em, especially the Pettijohns and Tutts and Gibsons.

3 *A frequent BYPT-er*

Just when Rev. Strickland was starting to think about stopping whatever he'd been saying ever since before my great-granddaddy was born, 'bout time I thought I would faint or at least die if he *didn't* let us out so I could get some air and get on down to the cafe. *All* I

was thinking about was what to wear to BTU
because somebody trying to beat my time with
Kenny Pettijohn. That's right—he my boyfriend
—he useta *think* he liked my cousin but now he
know it's me. He say it was me he was loving
all the time, reason I had to write that other girl a
note: "Kenny don't like you. He like me. sign
Kittie." Ain't nobody said nothing about getting
married! I ain't but fifteen but I do know plenty
people getting married at 14, and some of 'em,
cause they had to. I ain't studyin what Winnie
Hazel nem saying: the Lord gone smack me for
kissing Kenny in church. I'm going to BTU. I
ain't missed one in three years and I can't wait til 6
p.m. so I can wear my new dress Momma bought
me yesterday on sale at Gold's.

4 Mr. G.

Hypocrites. Liars & hypocrites.
Trying to act like they better'n everybody else.
Preacher going with any woman he can, married or not.
Grown, *old* women just come to show off new clothes.
Everybody badmouths each other. Know they can't stand
each other. Like this one person. I ain't calling no names
but every time she gets mad at somebody on Soque she
will walk out Second Street then down Cox, *back* out First
and around to Soque to get downtown, so everybody can
see how mad she is. But every Sunday—mad or not—she
right up in church with the rest. Hypocrites. I don't fool
with 'em. Anyway, me,
I'm a Methodist.

5 Two True Believers

I go to both
churches. Don't care
what they say, it's all the same, if
you serving God,
it's all the same.

              *

Yes it was the same
every 3rd or 4th Sunday
in summer when
the churches would have
big *spreads* of food when the ladies
made something special,
brought it to church and everybody
ate good. Reeeal good.   For free.

Sally's Cafe

Every Sunday after morning service,
they go to Sally's like the sermon sent them.
You might burn in
hell for your sins but you'd
go to Sally's first like
the Saturday nighters came to hang
over bacon eggs & grits, glazed
eyes with a smile leftover from last night
while good church folk walked self-
righteously in to condemn what they'd done
a few years   or hours   before.
Young folk came waiting to
grow up, get a ride to Mt. Airy, to
Fred's Tavern every day but Sunday.

> *put on yo high heel sneakers*
> *cause we steppn out tonight*
> *put on yo high heel sneakers*
> *we steppn out tonight . . .*

—you gone put on some clothes?
—might's well.
—well, I'll meet you at the top
    of the hill, about 8.

> *put on yo red dress, baby*
> *we steppn out tonight . . .*

put on some clothes and step
down the hill, down Soque and around the corner to
the cafe. Sally's Lunchroom, after
she moved it *up* the hill,
on Soque, but before that, it was
the Cafe. One big room, in back of their house.
One big room with a raggedy driveway to

walk up or a path behind
Mr. Miller's to get to (and before Sally, her daddy's place)
one big room, in an old brown wood
house with one pay telephone for everybody on the hill,
a jukebox with the latest hits,
especially James Brown's (a friend of Sally's)
and Sally and her husband Mr. Jack cooking.

That's where they went,
when they dressed up
to dance, to wait, to see
who might come up from Gainesville or
Toccoa looking good for each other

"Did you see him? Did you see
that husband yet? How he *look?*
Where he from, anyway?"

—He don't look like he got good sense.
—He look *good* to me.
—I can *see* why she married him!
—Did you hear her talk?
—I ain't seen him yet.
—He down to the café now.
—Let's go see him.

Some came *just* to style,
to be there, be admired or
more, just to dance, try a new
fancystep, eat fried mullet sandwiches with
mustard. Somebody played "Blue Moon"
over and over. A few waited for someone
to start woofing at somebody and
Miz Sally was *known* to put
them out: "Take that outta here.
Y'all take that foolishness out of here."
and the ones who came to dance,
steady dancing as Ethel Mae waits for a phone call
from Gainesville and

Mr. Papa Doc Williams

(1877–1984)

When I died I *was* the oldest man living in Cornelia even if
by then I didn't live in Cornelia, I did. I do. At the top of the
hill, at 121 Soque Street.

Haints can't hurt you. Whether I *believe* in them or not makes
no dif. They can't hurt you. And anyway, they was in this house
before I got here. Plus, I was through running. From haints or
anything else.

Came up here before there *was* a here, from Wilkes County me
and my wife and a few of my oldest kids. Round 19 and 15
or so, might have been. Thought I would have to keep
on moving, else kill somebody, til these crackers got it through
their head my wife is colored, same as me. Tried to lynch me
first though. Huh.
I was tired. And I was through running. I say, I was through
with running—that kind, anyhow. Found a little place, back in
the woods. Not many people out there but us, Dub King's and a
few more. Called it Dogtown, then. And after a while I moved
down here on the hill. Half these people my kin, or kin
to my kin, one.

Yes, I have seen some things. With my own eyes and even after
I lost my sight I seen more than *you* ever will. Knowed ever one
of my peoples too, even when I couldn't see 'em. My daughter
Lean tried to sneak up on me and one of my grands, Becky.
They never did and Lean never was right in the head, even if she
is my own daughter, especially after she married John Gibson's
oldest boy. Had to be crazy, to marry him. John's kids and mine
would fight each other every day. Soon's they saw each other,
they'd throw rocks til they got close enough to hit with they fists.
Reckon Jack hit Lean in the head with a rock. Guess she
thought it was a love tap. "Doc"

ain't my real name either, but you can't find nobody to tell you
different. And I ain't gone tell you different either. No

Demorest ain't the only place and you know it ain't. When they
run off (or killed off) all the Indians in Georgia, they started right
in on us! But me—I'm hard to kill! Lost one of my legs, lost my
eyesight—didn't matter. I *still* lived longer than most people
do, and I *did* some living. I died
when I got ready to.
I was not "passing through" here, like Clio said.
I was running. And when I got to Dogtown, after I stopped
laughing, I stopped running.

Miz Zelma (Shankle) Crow
(September 28, 1908–June 29, 1989)

If you hush and listen to anybody
besides yourself sometimes, you'd do better.
(Be better off and I b'lieve you'd
look better too.) Where we came from don't make a
bit of difference in this world—don't care what Doc
Williams say. Not by now, it don't. He talking
about Wilkes County—well, they wont no different in
Chicago, either. You pay attention now: it's some
people done forgot they human. You got to make them
remember. It's some of us like that too. Yes it is.
Yes it is. Right here on the hill.   Like my second husband.

People *will* try you. But Zelma Crow don't take nothing
off nobody. Clio? Naw, she never did try
to mess with *me.* I knowed 'em
when they lived in Banks County. One time, she asked
if I wanted—well, I didn't. And what she did, had
already been done. Before she came here, the Indians
owned all of this, all of Georgia. Owned some of us, too.
Oh yes, they did too. I told Clio. Don't trouble the spirits and
they will leave you alone. Remember that.
Because *some* spirits is spiteful. Spiteful
as the day is long. They don't mess
with Zelma Crow, neither.

Clio (continued)

They would be passing through,
coming from everywhere.
Never could see why they came but
they stayed because they had to.

Take Elvie. Her people came outta
Hollywood. She was a big-boned healthy
young woman, could see Indian blood in her
skin. Put me in the mind of
my Dina, sometimes, Elvie did.
I could *see* why
a man would want her but
not why she wanted the one she married,
kept having babies with. One day she
stood tall and straight. Next day, look like she
shrunk and had twelve children and a slew of grands.
Doubled all into herself, bloated up
and dipping snuff! I felt sorry for her being
married to John. A rounder. 8 to 80, blind
cripple, crazy—if it was female, well. That's how he was.
Even come trying to grin in *my* face (and this in church)
and all the while, Elvie steady having babies.

so *many* of them

the best you
can do is just
say one of Elvie's & John's
or ask
"which one *is* you?" Even
then, you won't be sure.

They made some pretty children,
John and Elvie did, moving from
house to house and finally to
the house down at the foot of
Soque Street next door to
Willie Hamilton—who had
a whole passel of kids herself,
come to think of it, and
then there was *Will* Gibson,
him and his wife Kate had kids;
they was Gibsons, too, but you wouldn't
mistake Kate's and Will's for
Elvie's and John's—it was
just confusing to tell *them*
apart. *Them* Gibsons.
Come to think of it I don't
believe they could always
tell themselves apart from
each other, half the time.
The other half, they'd just
be guessing.

Betty, Miz Zelma's granddaughter

(also Becky's cousin, Fish's niece, Miz Didley's daughter, Early
Wilmont Williams' ex-wife, Sue's sister-in-law, Barbara nem's
momma, and Poncie's baby's grandma)

"I ain't no kin to Winnie Hazel and
Sue. Hell no, I ain't kin to the Gibsons.
What? *What?* Buster might be my brother—
he married Sue. He kin to Sue. I ain't no kin
to no Gibsons. And I ain't no goddam kin to
everybody on the hill. No, I ain't. Hell no,
I ain't. And don't try to
goddam claim me, either."

Mr. Garland Cook

"What's so good about it?
About being home?
I just wondered what you'd say
and, this was before your time, but
about fifty years ago, I came to Cornelia.
I said a man would have to be a fool
to live here! I hated it.
Look at me now.
Fifty years later, I'm still here.
And I love it."

Death on Soque Street

Might be, somebody *could* tell the Gibsons apart but
they was all crazy. Some quiet-crazy some
loud-crazy, but still crazy. Like, how can you tell Will
from John Gibson? Because Will got a right hand full of nubs,
fingers all chopped off at the joint. John—his brother—
cut 'em off with an ax when they was little boys. Will said he didn't
believe John would. John said, "Lay 'em on the block."
Will did, and John did.
See what I mean? CRAZY.

Also, liars. The Gibsons, and anybody on the hill would help
a lie get started. Turn "looked like" into
"hope God may kill me" in a heartbeat.
They lied like they did everything else.
All together.

Could be a 1957 orange and white Mercury
heading across the hill, late one night (might be Baby June saw; he see
everything) moving sneaky because the driver worked for
a company who'd fire you for riding a woman besides y'r wife. Say it's a
weeknight—so make it eleven o'clock since the driver got to be to work
at seven next morning—and that car is creeping on in. Somebody might get
up (most folk asleep except Baby June) to pee. Hear something and look
out just to be nosey. By seven next morning, everybody would know who
she *thought* she saw. By the time the veneer plant whistle blowed
at 12 noon they'd be done made it a *fact*.

They got more ways of lying than
treeing a possum or cooking greens. Just set up—ain't got
nothing else to do—and
make up a lie, like Mack Gibson and that casket.

"Wouldn't it be something," he said, "if somebody's casket
rolled out of Shady Grove Church. Got fed up with
Rev. Strickland's hollering (plus, they'd heard it all
before) and just rolled on down the hill headed
out to Level Grove Cemetery. Wouldn't that be something?" Mack said.

Next thing I know, he's down there
on Soque telling his sisters and cousins he saw it.
Two days later, they swore they saw it too. I know
what I'm talking about. I was there.
I seen it too, rolling down
the hill one dark night, about 11:30.

Cycles

Regulated by the whistle
blowing time at the veneer plant
cycles of sunsets blown on a whistle
the mountains
in endless seasons, spring to
fall blown each year
winter encircling the hill in ice
regular concentric circles of
irregular spiral lives

Legacy

Nose in the air like you stink or
head down, admiring themselves.
That's what some people say and
maybe it's so but they can't help it.

Elvira Gibson walked on her toes, like
she was tipping. Her mind someplace
else, a little smile or frown on her face.
Maybe she got that—looking down—from
being stared at so hard. When she was a girl?
Prettiest in Habersham County.
Liked to dance and loved walking, just
going for long walks. Walked like she
was floating or dancing, light, light
on her feet all her life and you know, she
never *did* learn how to drive a car.

John, now. John was a hoss of a
different color. He was a good-looking man,
always talking about somebody had a
"million dollar grin" (like he knowed what a
million looked like). He had a $50 grin
himself. John was *always* grinning at
something, a story he had to tell, some
foolishness—and he walked straight, with
his head held high looking for somebody to
tell it to. (His brother Will walked and grinned
like that and *his* kids too. They
all Gibsons, ain't they?) That's why their
children walk like that. They got it honest
from Elvie and John.

The Gibsons, strolling

They took their time. Like they had all
the time in the world, at least all day.
They *took* their time and made it
worth your time to watch them. *All* of
them, girls and boys. Head held high or
dropped from the neck. Spine straight,
a rhythm from the waist
arms and hips swing slightly as their
feet slide along like the *feet* know
where they going and *they* just followed.

Summer, so hot tar melted, stuck to
your feet, between your toes. Even then
barefooted, they strolled and when they
spoke, John's grin came out. So many big
white teeth, it hurt your eyes. And here
they come.

Up and down the hill like it was there
just to give them practice. And what's
so bad about it, all them got that
walk! The grands and great-grands,
what I mean! Just to see 'em, any of
'em, put you in the mind of good
weather and good times when
they got wherever they was going. I mean—it
made you feel good, just to see them walk!

And that's why, or partly why, that
Trimiar boy, James, never had a chance.
That, and that brand new white 1963
Stingray he was driving.

The Summer of 1963 : James & Gladys

James was definitely one of the ones who left. Stayed gone and made something of himself, he did. That year when he came home, he was one of the Green Beret, the Special Forces, and he *wore* that beret and the rest of his army clothes like he was *born* in uniform and although some women just love men in uniforms, I never saw it, until I saw James. And then, I saw they point. He looked *good.* And knew it.

He was a little short man but sharp, in uniform or out. A nice regular brown with a little mustache. Nice smile, pretty little white teeth and good manners, even if he didn't say much but his whole family, the Trimiars, was like that, mostly kept to themselves. Their sister Irene too, but when James came home that summer she suddenly got a best buddy—I'll get to that in a minute.

And so. James came home and people couldn't get enough of looking at him. Many times as they saw that car, when they saw it again, they stared. James took a few folk for a ride (which I would *not* have done). They *really* talked—how they was *bound* to get them a car just like it and everybody speculated how much it cost; some *asked* him but he just smiled, never said. Yet, and still, everybody knew he was single.

Never been married and never had a girlfriend in Cornelia that we knowed of. So a lot of young girls (and some not so young) was just dying to give him some, already figgered out how to do it, in that teeninchy car. Sally got a *lot* of bizness every time James parked at the cafe, even when he parked across the street at 103 Soque.

Where she saw him? Most like, going in or out of Sally's. She liked what she saw, and once Gladys set her mind on something, that was that. Gladys. One of the lighter skinned-ed ones, took after her momma's side of the family. She had that walk, with some extra throwed in—her nose tilted up a little higher.

She was short, on the plump side, steady eating Argo starch—which I useta love, myself— and red dirt. Always fighting off blackheads and pimples. If you surprised her, she'd be *covered* with Noxzema but still and all, she was a good-looking young woman. And for years, her mind was set on Willis, her beau—well, when he wasn't with Charity's girl, Maggie Lean. Until that summer. Then, Gladys forgot the starch, the red dirt, *and* Willis.

Courtship at 103 Soque

All over the beatup furniture, people
in the front room, on the porch coming &
going, watching tv, eating, dancing,
talking, laughing, fighting but
Gladys cleared it out!
Made 'em all stay back in the kitchen, or
the other bedroom and they   better
not even   breathe.   Much less make noise.

Miz Elvie helped clean (I swear, she *painted*
the front room, so it'd look good
for one night). Covered the tables with
little lace thingies from one of Elvie's white women.
Found two *matching* lamps, put
a reg'lar lightbulb in one, and a red one in the other.
The front room tried to look like
a picture in one of the magazines Gladys
studied so much, and she looked like a 1950s
movie star—in her mind, anyhow,
for her comp'ny James.
Soon, they was engaged.
Then, instead of repeating
how "cute" he was, Gladys
had to convince you (and her) that
James couldn't hold Willis
against her. After all, they'd
only done it one time. She thought she had
James thinking she was a virgin. I swear 'fo God.
(Don't believe me, ask Anne.)
James *never* had   a   chance.

"Sgt. & Mrs." she practiced signing her name.
It's a wonder she didn't just write
"Mrs. Green Beret Special Forces White 1963 Stingray."
She was just *that* happy. Just
that proud.

those lamps

bottom of brown and
green plastic painted
like a tree. The shade of
tin, red tin shingles
of small circles getting
bigger as they went down.
Plastic and tin, painted red,
with little gold colored chains
holding the red tin circles
together.

The *ugliest* lamps   in
the world. It's a wonder
they didn't scare James off
or that he didn't shoot them.
Probably, they put him in
some kind of *transfer* so
he didn't know what was what.
In shock, what he was.

Gladys & Irene

Gladys had personality though. Have to give her that—
you'd have thought Lloyd Price
wrote that song about her.
She was still stuck up. Acted
like she better than everybody. *Plenty*
girls looked way better'n her.
She was sneaky and conniving and I'm
just telling the truth. Look how she did Irene.
Hardly spoke to her before James—but after that!
Stuck to Irene like white on rice. Sure, Irene
was glad but you could see she was kinda dazed.
Gladys *Gibson?* All her and Gladys had in common
was high school, a few extra pounds,
and James—who Irene had, by blood,
and who Gladys *meant* to have, by blood, if it came to
that. (Irene never was fast, like Gladys.)

Irene couldn't hardly *breathe* for Gladys. Good thing
she hurried up and got engaged to James. Then,
she dropped Irene cold. Before that, she tried to fix
Irene up with her brother (called him "Kookie," for some
odd reason). James T. saved his sister's life. Otherwise,
Gladys woulda sucked it all out of her. She was just one
selfish, sneaky b——.
And don't you believe what these folk be saying
about me. I know somebody done told you
I wanted James. They liars, all of 'em. Full of spite and
lies, and God gone slap 'em all silly one day!

Gladys Parlee Gibson Trimiar

(August 16, 1944–April 9, 1986)

I always had a taste for finer things.
They were all jealous, even before
James dated me.

My competition was in France, Germany,
Massachusetts, Vietnam *and* Cornelia.
He wasn't here long, I didn't have
much time. He was older than me—but all the
books say that's how it should be,
older men like young girls. So I had some fast,
hard work to do. And when I finished,
James was crazy about me. Me? Never
had it so good, girl! I had everything I wanted
and things *were* cheaper, on Post. And the
traveling was so *much* fun! Even after I
realized that James had bad habits (like other
women) he didn't plan to change. But that was
much later.

I lay here now, *knowing*
I made other plans near the end,
and I know, if I had it to do again,
I'd do the same.
Pu-leese. I did what most women
would have; if I got to him before them
—well, good for me. And another thing.

He was not *that* tired
and I didn't look that good
(though I *was* looking good).
It wasn't my new diet *or* the Noxzema.
Not the lamps either, silly.
It was Miz Clio. I did what *she*
told me and I got what I wanted. Period.

Tanya Davenport

(1955–1971)

All y'all funny, to me. You ought to listen to *us*
but you won't.
Ought to hear what *we* saying,
but you don't know how. No,

that pain in my head and
neck stopped a long time ago
except when I laugh so hard my head hurts.
(That bad eczema on my foot
cleared up too.) Now, I *know* I can
tell some things. Me and the others
float on the hill seeing you like you
look at television. We do what we want to.
Every now and then, I *do* want a cold
Pepsi-Cola. Momma
puts cartons of Pepsi under the sink.
Wonders why she spills so many,
why it's less there, says,
"I could *swear* I bought
more than that." But I don't mean
no harm. Just having a little laugh,
a little fun. We *don't*
mean no harm, but
we mean *something*. Miz Clio loves a good
joke and she's laughed a lot about—
but not now. Learn to hear us.
Then maybe I'll tell you.

Ceremony

New Orleans streets. Rich in song,
story, madness, voodoo & magic.
Not, however, the only place. Still,
seems like it's allrighter there. Other
places, you got to get permission. Well, i got
permission, now.
Now, i got a permit.

Soquee is a Cherokee word *for* the Hill,
cross the railroad track, in Appalachian foothills,
where madness runs like the Chattahoochee River.
Like kudzu in the mind.

Sak-wi Yi.   Sounds inflected
in rhythmical air
in a sacred place.

Don't mess with the sacred.
It *will* get you.